WORLD WAR I
IN PHOTOGRAPHS

WORLD WAR I
IN PHOTOGRAPHS

SERIES EDITOR PAUL WHITTLE

EAGLE EDITIONS

Acknowledgements

Thanks are due to the following people for making this book possible: Thomas Mitchell for picture research; Andrew Webb at the Robert Hunt Library for his indefatigable search for the right pictures; Hulton Getty Images Ltd; Matthew Smith and all at Arcuturus, rising star in the publishing firmament; Jonathan Watts, inspirational historian; Heike Becker for being there; Annette Krzyworaczka, for being the best.

Published by Eagle Editions Limited
11 Heathfield, Royston, Hertfordshire SG8 5BW

Published 2003

© Arcturus Publishing Limited
26/27 Bickels Yard
151–153 Bermondsey Street
London SE1 3HA

Series jacket design by Alex Ingr
Designed and Typeset by Mike Harrington,
MATS Typesetting

ISBN 1-84193-192-6

Printed and bound in China

Contents

The Roots of Conflict

AT THE OUTSET OF 1914, the nations of Europe were divided into two major power blocs: the Central Powers of Germany and Austria-Hungary, and a rather looser alliance of France, Russia and Great Britain.

Immediately following the Franco-Prussian War of 1870–1871, the German Chancellor, Otto von Bismarck, had proclaimed the birth of a unified Germany.

Although the emergence of this new 'super-state' was viewed with some alarm by the other European powers, the diplomatic status quo had been maintained by Bismarck through an intricate network of treaties and alliances, which pacified the European

Archduke Franz Ferdinand, heir to the throne of the Habsburg emperors of Austria, together with his wife enters the Serbian town of Sarajevo on his ill-fated visit of 28 June 1914. The date was particularly unfortunate, as it was the anniversary of a fourteenth-century Turkish victory over Serbia, and still then a source of national humiliation to the Serbs.

powers while leaving the way open for Germany to achieve her newly-awakened dreams of Empire by peaceful means.

With the accession of Kaiser Wilhelm II to the German throne in 1888, however, the situation had changed. The antithesis to the coolly logical Bismarck, Wilhelm was determined to make Germany a world power by any means necessary, an approach which had soon alienated Russia and Great Britain, and left Germany the Austro-Hungarian empire as her sole ally in Europe. Austria-Hungary, however, had problems of her own. The rise of Slav nationalism in her southern provinces, encouraged by a Russia keen to expand her own influence in the Balkan region, was threatening the stability of the empire itself. At the urging of the Army chief of staff Major General Conrad von Hötzendorf, the Austrian empire prepared to crush Serbia, viewed by the Austrian government as the instigator of the Slav demands for independence. All Hötzendorf needed was an excuse. That excuse came as the heir to the Habsburg throne, Archduke Franz Ferdinand paid a state visit to the Serbian capital of Sarajevo on 28 June 1914. As the Archduke's driver was attempting to find his way back from the official reception, a young Serbian nationalist named Gavrilo Princip stepped forward and fired into the car, killing the Archduke and his wife, and earning himself a footnote in history. The Austrian response came on 23 July, and consisted of a series of outrageous demands on the Serb government, including a demand not only that Austrian officials be involved in the Serbian investigation into the assassination, but also in the judicial process following any arrests. This demand proved to be the sticking-point for the Serbs, as the Austrians had known that it would. Backed by Germany, Austria envisaged a short war, resulting in an end to Slav demands for independence. The complex network of treaties which had maintained the peace in Europe, however, now ensured that the conflict, once begun, would not remain localised for long.

Opening Moves

THE FIRST MOVE of the 'Great War', as the First World War would be known until the advent of the Second, was made by the Austro-Hungarian Empire. After Serbia had failed to comply absolutely with the purposefully impossible terms of the Austrian ultimatum of 23 July, Austria broke off diplomatic relations on 25 July, following this with a declaration of war on 28 July. The conflict had officially begun, although it was by no means inevitable that Germany and Russia, allies of the belligerent nations, would become involved. As late as midday on 28 July, Kaiser Wilhelm was writing that in his opinion the Serbian reply to the Austrian ultimatum had 'removed all reason for war', and that any remaining questions could easily be solved by diplomacy. As Austrian river craft began the bombardment of Belgrade on 29 July, however, Russia felt impelled to mobilise her army in support of the beleaguered Serbs, leading in turn to full German mobilisation in support of Austria. Once these military machines were set in motion, it became almost impossible to stop them as they acquired a momentum all of their own. France refused a German demand to undertake to remain neutral in the event of hostilities between Germany and Russia, instead embarking on a general mobilisation of her own. The British remained non-committal, agreeing to support neither one side nor the other, partly in the hope that war would be averted, and partly because many in Britain felt that it was not their concern if the nations of Europe went to war.

▲ The arrest of Gavrilo Princip (right, between two policemen) in Sarajevo immediately after his assassination of Franz Ferdinand.

As Russia persisted in her mobilisation, rejecting German demands to demobilise, the German Empire declared war on Russia on 1 August, following this two days later on 3 August by a declaration of war against France.

At the beginning of August 1914, then, a European war was officially underway, with Austria-Hungary and Germany on the one hand, and Serbia, Russia and France on the other. Despite having alliances with both France and Russia, Britain had not yet entered the fray. Germany was a traditional British ally, despite recent tensions caused by the German build-up of naval power, and neither the *Entente Cordiale* with France, nor the Triple Alliance with France and Russia obliged the British to go to war in support of her treaty partners.

◆ Serbian peasant led away for interrogation by Austrian troops, 1914. The invading Austrian army quickly acquired a reputation for brutality amongst the Serbian populace.

◆ Serbian troops retreat across the marshes at Scutari, 1914.

The British declaration of war on Germany would come on 4 August, and would stem from a circumstance no one had taken into account: the German violation of Belgian neutrality.

The Schlieffen Plan

The understandable German reluctance to wage war on two fronts simultaneously had led in 1905 to the creation of the Schlieffen Plan, named after its creator General Alfred von Schlieffen. The aim of this plan was to avoid the two-front war by a swift defeat of France in the West, within forty days, followed by a transfer of troops to the Eastern Front, there to pursue a more leisurely campaign against a Russia who would almost certainly be slow to fully mobilise her troops. This, then, was the German plan of attack in 1914.

Unfortunately, the plan depended for its success on the right wing of the attacking German armies being able to advance through Belgium, and Belgium was neutral. Belgium also intended to stay neutral, and refused the German armies permission to pass through her territory. When the Germans violated that neutrality, Britain issued an ultimatum of her own, citing the 1839 Treaty of London which guraranteed Belgian neutrality, and demanding that all German forces be withdrawn. When a withdrawal was not forthcoming, Britain declared war on Germany.

◆ German troops cross the border into Belgium, violating Belgian neutrality.

The British army of the time, however, was essentially a colonial police force: professional and well-trained, but above all small; no more than 150,000 men, in contrast to the German army of over 4 million, 1.5 million of whom were deployed on the Western Front in August 1914. On 7 August, therefore, Lord Kitchener, Secretary of State for War, issued an appeal for 100,000 men to join the British army. The ensuing crowds outside recruiting offices were so huge that mounted

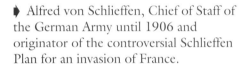

▶ Alfred von Schlieffen, Chief of Staff of the German Army until 1906 and originator of the controversial Schlieffen Plan for an invasion of France.

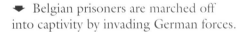

➤ Belgian prisoners are marched off into captivity by invading German forces.

police had to be called to keep order, and special outdoor recruiting offices were set up around the country. By the end of the year, well over one million men had enlisted. The mood across Britain, and indeed across much of Europe, was that this was simply a 'great adventure', and that it 'would all be over by Christmas'. This mood, however, does not wholly account for the success of the recruiters; by the end of 1915, when it was clear to all that the war in fact would not be over for some time to come, the number had risen to over 2.5 million.

◆ Perhaps the most famous image of the First World War, Kitchener's posters were part of a massive campaign to mobilise Britain's civilian population.

◆ Following Lord Kitchener's appeal for soldiers, regular recruiting stations found themselves inundated, leading to the setting up of emergency stands, such as this one in London's Trafalgar Square.

◆ Recruits of the Lincolnshire Regiment practise rifle drill, September 1914. The original age range for Kitchener's Army was set between 19 and 30, with the upper limit soon increased to 35.

Breaching Belgian Neutrality

Meanwhile on the Continent, the war was moving ahead apace. Austro-Hungarian troops invaded Serbia on 12 August, dogged by many reports of atrocities committed against the local Serb population; similar incidents would be reported amongst the German troops occupying Belgium, including the burning of the city of Louvain, along with the priceless book collection held in its library. These reports outraged public opinion across the world, and Allied propaganda was not slow to take advantage of this.

On 16 August the Belgian forts of Liege finally fell, as the Germans opened fire with heavy railway guns such as Big Bertha. Although the small and antiquated Belgian army was being pushed back across the entire country, it was nevertheless resisting fiercely, long enough for the British Expeditionary Force, which had arrived in Belgium on 11 August under its commander General Sir John French, to arrive at Mons on 20 August. At this time, the BEF consisted of two army corps, I Corps under the command of Lieutenant-General Sir Douglas Haig, and II Corps under General Sir Horace Smith-Dorrien, and the Cavalry Corps under General Sir Edward Allenby, who would later make his name in the Middle East.

The first encounter between British and German troops took place on 22 August, when a detachment of the Royal Irish Dragoon Guards encountered German soldiers from the 4 Kurassier Regiment. The British opened fire, killing several and capturing a number of prisoners. These were the first shots fired in anger on the continent of Europe by British troops in a century.

➥ Recruits line up outside the Royal Engineers' barracks at Chatham in Kent.

The Battle of Mons

At Mons, the small British force was confronted by units of the German First and Second armies under General Alexander von Kluck and Field Marshal Karl von Bülow respectively. The British took up their positions at Nimy, just to the north of Mons itself, along the south side of the canal, defending the four bridges that were concentrated in the area. Early in the morning of 23 August, the Germans appeared, heading south towards the British positions, and the British opened fire. The British held the line of the Mons Canal throughout the day, but with the withdrawal of the French Fifth Army under General Lanrezac, the position became untenable, and the troops were forced to retreat. The first Victoria Crosses of the war were awarded to Lieutenant M.J. Dease and Private Frank Godley for covering the British retreat at Nimy with their machine gun. When Dease was injured, Godley took over, and held up the Germans on his own for over an

➤ One of the metal cupolas of the Belgian fortress of Namur lies smashed by German artillery. Believed by the Belgians to be invulnerable to artillery fire, the massive guns developed by the German firm of Krupps would prove to be simply too heavy to withstand.

☛ Belgian troops put up barricades outside the town of Louvain, 20 August 1914, and await the invading Germans during the retreat to Antwerp.

◆ A German horse-drawn transport column passes through the almost deserted streets of Brussels, 26 August 1914. Although both sides would make huge advances in weaponry throughout the war, the speed of their advances would continue to be dictated by the speed of a horse-drawn wagon.

◆ The retreat from Mons: British cavalry begin the long journey back to the outskirts of Paris from Mons, August, 1914. Although the Cavalry Corps under General Allenby fought well, they were essentially a nineteenth-century formation in what would rapidly become a twentieth-century conflict.

hour. Eventually he was overwhelmed, whereupon he threw his machine gun into the canal and was taken prisoner.

Although the Battle of Mons was little more than a local skirmish, resulting in around 1,500 casualties for the British and around 5,000 for the Germans, it held up the advancing German First Army and gave the Allies valuable breathing space, as did the battle three days later at Le Cateau. However, the British and the French were retreating; in good order, but retreating nonetheless, a long and arduous retreat which would take them back to a line that began to the north-east of Paris, where the newly-formed French Sixth Army was holding the line, flanked by the BEF holding positions which curved round south along the line of the Seine. The Allied front line then crossed the Marne and went north to the great French fortress of Verdun, held by the French Third Army, then snaked south behind Nancy and to the east of Epinal, held by the French Second and First Armies. These armies, in attempting to carry out the French Plan XVII for the capture of Alsace-Lorraine and the push to the Rhine had met only defeat, at Morhange, and then at Sarrebourg, and had been forced back onto French soil by the German Fifth, Sixth and Seventh armies.

This new line proved defensible, and it was from here that the French commander, General Joseph Joffre launched the counter-attack, which broke the German lines, and pushed them back up to 60 miles in places, as far as the high ground along the River Aisne, where they took up their new positions. The Allies also began to dig in, and the long war of attrition began.

Belgian soldiers fight a rearguard action after blowing up a railway bridge at Termonde, covering the retreat to Antwerp, 18 September 1914.

The Eastern Front

The Russian attack on East Prussia on 17 August took the Germans, who were expecting Russian mobilisation to take much longer, by surprise. The initial offensive saw the Russians defeat the weak German forces in East Prussia at Gumbinnen on 20 August. The German withdrawal to Königsberg was orderly, however, and gave them time to regroup as the exhausted Russians ground to a halt. Under the leadership of General Paul von Hindenburg, and Major General Erich Ludendorff, the German forces split the First and Second Russian armies, surrounding the Second and forcing it to surrender in what became known as the Battle of Tannenberg, even though it actually took place at nearby Frogenau. German advances on Warsaw were repulsed by the Russians, who counter-attacked around Silesia in November, but were eventually forced to withdraw to around Warsaw once more. As the weather on the Eastern Front worsened, both sides dug in and prepared to wait out the winter.

The Race to the Sea

On the Western Front, both sides had dug in to the west of Paris, following the Battle of the Marne. From these positions, they began to try and outflank the other in the east, in order to catch the enemy between two fires. This series of outflanking moves became known, misleadingly, as the 'race to the sea'. By mid-October, the line of trenches had crossed the

⬆ French artillery spotter at the First Battle of the Marne, September 1914. Artillery would come to play an ever more important role in the First World War, as the techniques for its use became more sophisticated.

◆ French troops advance through a village on their way to the front line, First Battle of the Marne.

Somme, the scene of so much bitter fighting in the years to come, and reached the Belgian coast at Nieuport, to the north of Dunkirk. The Germans attacked the British salient around Ypres, hoping that a breakthrough here would lead them on to the channel ports of Calais and Dunkirk. Once these were in German hands, the task of supplying the BEF would become almost impossible. The attack opened on 20 October, and lasted more or less continuously until the middle of November. The Germans poured men into the attack, desperate to gain a success that could bring the war to a close. The British, however, reinforced by Indian Army troops, held fast. By the end of the battle, Wytschaete, Gheluvelt and Ploegsteert had all been taken by the Germans, and would remain in German hands for much of the war.

As 1914 drew to a close, the front line extended from the North Sea to the Swiss border: little was to change over the next four years.

◀ German infantry soldier lies dead on the Marne.

☝ Rifles poised and at the ready, French infantry hold the bank of a canal on the Western Front, September 1914.

☝ French cavalry move up to the attack at the Marne. Generals on both sides found it hard to recognise that the trenches of the Western Front were no place for cavalry charges.

◆ German troops snatch what sleep they can in their firing positions in the front line, First Battle of the Aisne, 1914.

◆ French cavalry and infantrymen survey the German positions on the Aisne, October 1914.

◆ The Battle of Tannenberg: German infantry advance against Russian shelling. The battle was actually fought at Frogenau, but Ludendorff, knowing that an ancestor of Hindenburg's had fought at an earlier Battle of Tannenberg in 1410, dated his victory despatch from that town. The name became synonymous with German feats of arms, and a memorial to Hindenburg would be erected on the site.

◆ Russian prisoners are led off into captivity by German infantrymen after the Battle of Tannenberg, East Prussia, August 1914.

➥ The Cloth Hall at Ypres burns during the German attack, October 1914. The German army lost almost 170,000 men killed, captured, wounded or missing during the First Battle of Ypres, a quarter of their losses in all their campaigns during 1914.

◀ 2ⁿᵈ Scots Guards lead a reconaissance in force towards Gheluvelt, 20 October. The Regimental drummer, Private Steer, would be killed near this spot, the first casualty of the First Battle of Ypres.

◀ Soldiers of the Oxford and Bucks Light Infantry shelter behind 17ᵗʰ Division's HQ at Ypres, October 1914.

▲ 129ᵗʰ Baluchi Division advancing to the British front line near Hollebeke Chateau at Ypres, 28 October 1914. The Indian Corps played a vital role in holding off the German Ypres offensive, losing 6,000 men in the process.

◀ The Poona Division takes ship at Bombay Dock on their way to the Mesopotamian front, October 1914.

➡ British and German troops fraternise during the Christmas truce of 1914. This fraternisation was soon stopped by senior officers on both sides, however, fearing, perhaps correctly, that soldiers would be reluctant to kill men they had met personally.

➤ The famous Christmas truce of 1914: this drawing by Gilbert Holliday, based on an eyewitness description, shows Scots and German troops either playing football, or joining in a hare hunt.

Digging In

O N THE WESTERN FRONT, the winter of 1914/1915 was spent by both sides extending their systems of trenches, although in very different ways due to the differing requirements of each side. The British trenches in particular were intended to serve as the springboard to attack, and were built with up to three lines of reserve trench, connected to the front line by a series of communication trenches. The German trenches, on the other hand, had been constructed with defence in mind, the German aim being to tie down the Western Front with as few men as possible, expending her main energies on winning the war with Russia, and only then to concentrate on the war in the west.

Throughout 1915, with the exception of the German attacks of the Second Battle of Ypres in April, the pattern would be one of Allied attacks and German defence. The first Allied offensive came in March, at Neuve Chapelle, where the intention was for Douglas Haig's troops, now

◆ Neuve Chapelle. British dead along the front line, Battle of Neuve Chapelle, March 1915. Although the ultimate aim of the attack, the capture of the Aubers Ridge, failed, Neuve Chapelle was secured at the end of the month and would remain in British hands until the German spring offensives of 1918.

designated as First Army, to move on the town of Neuve Chapelle, and from there capture the Aubers Ridge beyond. After an artillery barrage kept necessarily brief due to a severe shortage of shells, the British were successful in taking the town, but could not keep the effort going, the advance troops outdistancing their communications and reserves. Although the town would remain in British hands, the real point of the battle of Neuve Chapelle, that a short artillery barrage could be extremely effective and take the enemy by surprise, was sadly forgotten.

The Anglo-French offensive in the Artois-Champagne areas would meet much the same result, with the Allies tactically unable to exploit their initial successes, and being pushed back by strong German counter-attacks. During the Battle of Loos, 25 September – 14 October, in which Rudyard Kipling's son John was killed, the Commander-in-Chief of the BEF Sir John French kept the British reserves some 16 miles behind the front lines, with the result that British gains could not be followed up. When the reserves finally did arrive in the front line, the opportunity had passed, and the subsequent piecemeal attacks simply cost the British more casualties. French was an experienced and able soldier, but was unable to grasp the huge changes warfare had undergone since the Boer War. French was replaced in December with Sir Douglas Haig, commander of the British First Army.

♠ German troops wearing improvised gas masks, Western Front, 1915. Although tear gas had been used in limited quantities, and to limited effect, on both fronts in 1914, the gas used by the Germans at Langemarck during the Second Battle of Ypres was the altogether more unpleasant chlorine, which in extreme cases destroyed the tissue of the lungs, in effect drowning the victim.

▶ German troops release chlorine gas, Ypres, 1915. The effectiveness of this type of attack depended entirely on which way the wind was blowing.

➡ The aftermath: street in the town of Loos after the battle. 'Tower Bridge', a pair of iron winding towers at the pit-head of the local mine, can be clearly seen in the background. One tower was destroyed in the fighting in September, the other a few months later.

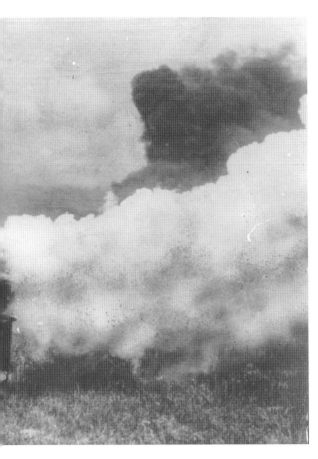

British infantry return from Loos, October 1915.

➤ Scots regiment returns from the line after the
Battle of Loos, October 1915.

➤ Battle of Loos, 25 September 1915. 'Tower
Bridge' can be seen to the centre-right of the picture

▲ Field Marshal Sir Douglas Haig.

🔹 Sir Douglas Haig arrives at Allied General Headquarters, to take up his new position as Commander-in-Chief of the British Expeditionary Force, 23 December 1915.

Sir John French, Commander-in-Chief of the British Expeditionary Force until December 1915. A distinguished cavalry commander, French struggled to come to grips with the demands of trench warfare, partly due to his concern for his men. He was replaced in December 1915 by General Haig.

The Home Front

After it had become clear that this was not a war which would be over by Christmas, the long process of maintaining an air of normality in the face of privation set in. Morale in Britain generally remained high, despite the attentions of the German air force, who made frequent bombing raids, firstly using Zeppelin airships, including the first air raid on London, 31 May 1915, and subsequently in Giant and Gotha

◆ Funeral of the victims of a Zeppelin air raid on London, 1915. The Zeppelins had first been used to drop bombs on Antwerp in Belgium during the invasion of 1914, and were regarded with dread by the populations of Allied cities.

➤ Church in Hull burns after a Zeppelin raid of June, 1915.

bombers. Food shortages, although common, did not become severe until German submarine warfare reached its height during 1917, when the government introduced a rationing system. The sense of 'fair play' that this generated was almost as important to the maintenance of civilian moral as the actual rationing itself, promoting as it did the idea that everyone 'was all in it together'.

Civilian morale was recognised by the British government as crucial to the war effort; the German government, on the other hand, subordinated everything to the requirements of the army, damaging their war effort.

➤ German naval airship L.53.

HAMPDEN HOUSE, LTD.

Beer Ration Card.

Name _Leslie Curnow_   Room _40.9._

Week ending _March 23_   _1918_

	LUNCHEON	DINNER
SUNDAY	½ Pint	½ Pint
MONDAY		
TUESDAY		
WEDNESDAY		
THURSDAY		
FRIDAY		
SATURDAY		

RATION.

1 PINT per day.

(far right)
achine gun and
ok out position
the outer
velope of a
rman Zeppelin.
e gunner would
a speaking tube
communicate
th the pilot.

Beer ration card,
ued to a Mr
slie Curnow.
e ration is a less-
n-princely one
t per day.

Anti-German riots
he East End of
ndon, 1915. Anti-
rman feeling ran
h at times during
war, especially
r the sinking of
Lusitania and
execution of
th Cavell, leading
ny families with
rmanic-sounding
nes, including the
ily Saxe-Coburg-
tha, to change
m.

Propaganda poster exhorting the British population to eat less bread. Campaigns like this one, organised centrally by the British government, had a huge impact.

The Gallipoli Campaign

Turkey had joined the war on the side of the Central Powers in 1914. In order to protect the vital Suez Canal, the Allies decided on an attack on Turkey direct, with the secondary purpose of keeping supply routes to Russia through the Dardanelles open. On 18 March, a joint Anglo-French naval bombardment began on Turkish positions in the Dardanelles, and on 25 April, an Allied force landed on the Gallipoli peninsula. This force consisted of around 60,000 men, half of whom were from the Australia and New Zealand Army Corps, the Anzacs. The aim was to capture the heights and then head north to deliver a knock-out blow on Istanbul. In the event, the attacks were plagued by the poor logistics so much in evidence on the Western Front, and Turkish resistance proved much stiffer than anticipated. The fighting continued, in a manner very like that of the Western Front, until finally the Allied troops were evacuated in December, having suffered over 250,000 casualties, with the Turks losing perhaps 300,000. This kind of landing, against a well-defended enemy shore, had never been attempted before, and in this instance, proved sadly beyond the Allies' technical and logistical skills.

➦ French battleships in action in the Dardanelles, March 1915. The naval attacks were unfortunately not followed up for a month, giving the Turkish defenders time to regroup and improve their defences.

◀ Transports for the Gallipoli expedition at Lemnos, April 1915.

➡ A view of 'V' Beach on Cape Helles at the southernmost tip of the Gallipoli peninsula. The British suffered appalling losses coming ashore here, comparable to those of the US at Omaha Beach during the Second World War.

▶ Anzacs – Australian and New Zealand Army Corps – on Gallipoli, May 1915. The Anzacs lost over 10,000 men during the eight-month Gallipoli campaign, and earned nine Victoria Crosses. As news of the mounting casualties filtered back home, recruitment in both countries increased in response. Anzac Day is celebrated on 25 April, the anniversary of the first landings on Gallipoli, and is a fitting tribute to the courage of the men who lost their lives there.

➥ Troops of the 5th Battalion of the Connaught Rangers take ship for Gallipoli, July 1915.

Turkish prisoners captured during the initial assault on Suvla Bay, 7 August 1915. Once again initial British successes were not followed up, with the result that the new landings suffered the same fate as the original ones.

Gunners of 52nd Division firing a 5-inch howitzer at Suvla, late 1915.

Kemal Ataturk, father of modern Turkey. As a corps commander, he would make a name for himself during the defence of Gallipoli.

➤ The British poet Rupert Brooke, who would die of septicaemia on the Greek island of Scyros, while waiting to embark for Gallipoli. His patriotic and inspiring poems may have been less so, had he lived to witness the slaughter on the Gallipoli peninsula.

The sinking of the *Lusitania* 7 May 1915

The Cunard liner *Lusitania* set sail from New York on 1 May 1915, with a complement of 2,000 passengers and crew. Six days later, she was sighted off the coast of Ireland by a German submarine, *U-20*, and promptly torpedoed, sinking within twenty minutes. This act outraged public opinion across the world, prompting anti-German riots which many governments did little to quell. Among the 1,200 drowned were 130 US citizens, shocking American public opinion. It was in part due to a resumption of unrestricted submarine warfare by the Germans that helped bring the US into the First World War.

◆ Survivors of the sinking of the *Lusitania* in Ireland, 7 May 1915.

◆ How the press reported the sinking of the *Lusitania*.

CRIME THAT HAS STAGGERED HUMANITY: THE TORPEDOING OF THE LUSITANIA

▶ German medal struck to commemorate the *Lusitania*, 1915. The medal suggests the sinking is the fault of the Cunard company, for ignoring the presence of German U-boats in the Atlantic. The legend at the top of the medal reads 'Business above all', the tickets are sold by the figure of Death, and a passenger in the queue reads a newspaper warning of the U-boat danger. This conveniently ignores the fact that all aboard the liner were non-combatants, and the fact that a liner is impossible to mistake for any other type of ship.

The Eastern Front

Mobility was much more a feature of the Eastern than Western Front, due mainly to the vast amounts of space and relative sparsity of troops (around 80 divisions on each side in the East, compared with over 100 in the West along a far shorter Western Front). The gains that were made, though, would prove almost as hard to keep .

The Austrians began the year with an assault on Russian positions in the Carpathians, attempting to relieve the siege of Premsyl. The attack was unsuccessful, and cost the Austrian army over 500,000 casualties. The Russian losses were also heavy, however, and they were heavier still when the German offensive north of the Masurian Lakes was launched on 7 February. The battles of Gorlice and Tarnow cost the Russians some 400,000 men: altogether the campaigning in 1915 cost Russia some two million men.

▲ Italian field gun in action, Isonzo Front, 1915. The fighting on this front would take place over the same ground time after time, until the German advance of November 1917 would drive the Italians back to the line of the Piave River.

The Italian Front

Despite being involved in alliances with Germany and Austria-Hungary, when Italy joined the war it was on the Allied side. After offering to join the Central Powers in return for territorial concessions from Austria on April 8, Italy then began negotiations with the Allies when the Austrians rejected this less-than-selfless offer. Led by the new commander-in-chief General Luigi Cadorna, the Italians launched three offensives during the course of 1915 against the Austrian positions to the east along the Caporetto–Monfalcone line, none of which were successful and cost the Italians around 125,000 casualties in all. This pattern would repeat itself throughout the war, until November 1917 when a combined Austrian-German assault would overwhelm the Italian defenders and force them back beyond the line of the Piave river.

☛ Constructing a pontoon bridge, on the Isonzo Front, 1915. Of the 615,000 troops Italy would lose in the First World War, the vast majority would be killed in this region.

Salonika

On 6 October, a combined attack by German, Austrian and Bulgarian troops was launched on Serbia, still holding out against the Austrian army more than a year after the beginning of the Austrian attack. The Serbs, hopelessly outnumbered and outgunned, were driven into a killing

◆ British cyclist company disembarks at Salonika, 2 November 1915.

retreat into Albania, during which an estimated 20,000 refugees perished from cold, hunger and bandit attacks. Allied landings at Salonika 5 October to bolster the Serbs came too little too late, and the only help they were able to provide was the evacuation of a large part of the Serb army from Albania in November.

British troops landing stakes, and fascines for the construction of defences, Salonika November 1915.

The Execution of Edith Cavell 12 October 1915

◆ Nurse Edith Cavell, shot on 12 October
1915 by the Germans for helping Allied
prisoners-of-war to escape. The execution
caused a huge swell of anti-German feeling
in Britain and the United States,
particularly after the circulation of the
(false) story that she had fainted on the
way to the execution post and had been
shot lying on the ground.

➤ Funeral cortege of Edith Cavell passes through London, when her body was returned by the
Germans, 15 May 1919. The *Times* reported that a 'wonderful stillness rested over the streets' as the
cortege made its way to Westminster Abbey.

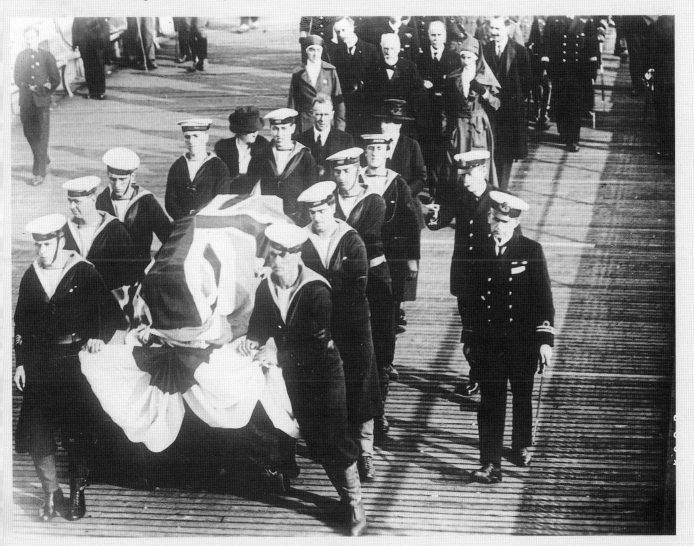

Deadlock

ON 6 DECEMBER, representatives of all Allied armies, British, French, Russian and Italian, met to discuss their strategy for the forthcoming year. In view of the fact that the Central Powers were fighting on three fronts, they decided on a series of co-ordinated assaults on all fronts. In the East, the Russians would attack through East Prussia, the Italians would attack again at Isonzo, while the assault on the Western Front would take place in Picardy, in the area to the north of the Somme river.

The Battle of Jutland 31 May 1916

The only large-scale naval battle of the First World War, the Battle of Jutland was a strategic victory for the Royal Navy, despite their losing more ships than the Germans. When Admiral Scheer decided to put the German High Seas Fleet out to sea, it was intercepted by Admiral Beatty's ships, based in the Firth of Forth. During the ensuing

◄ Admiral Beatty's flagship *Lion* is shelled and the battlecruiser *Queen Mary* is destroyed at the Battle of Jutland, 31 May 1916.

▶ British battlecruiser *Lion* is hit on a turret by a German salvo.

long-range duel Beatty's flagship *Lion* was damaged, and the battlecruiser *Queen Mary* was sunk. When the remainder of the British fleet arrived from their base in Scapa Flow, however, the Germans quickly withdrew, aware that they ran the risk of utter destruction if they continued to engage. The German fleet would not leave port in large numbers again.

➤ Loss of the battlecruiser *Queen Mary*.

➤ The German Fleet is deflected from bombarding the British coast by Admiral Beatty's battle cruiser squadron, who form a protective screen during the Battle of Jutland.

The Battle of Verdun

In the event, the British and French were pre-empted by a German attack on the fortress of Verdun. Verdun was a city of almost mythical importance to the French, and Falkenhayn believed that they would throw everything into its defence. His brutally simple plan was to draw the French into a killing ground, and, in his phrase, 'bleed them white'.

On 21 February, after a preliminary bombardment lasting 21 hours, one million German troops opened the offensive at Verdun. Initially, the Germans enjoyed huge success, taking the fort at Douaumont, and a considerable area of ground. However, the French, under their new commander Marshal Philippe Petain, held the line, and the Germans failed to capture the vital high ground around Verdun. They had underestimated the substantial reorganisation of the French defences, the strength of the French artillery, and perhaps most importantly the French fighting spirit. Attack after attack came to nothing, and all the while the French artillery was turning the entire area into a quagmire, the likes of which would become horribly familiar to the British at Passchendaele the following year. Ultimately at Verdun, the Germans bled more than the French, a state of affairs which would lead to Falkenhayn's replacement by Hindenburg and Ludendorff. The pressure on the French defenders at Verdun was unrelieved throughout the early half of 1916, however, and it was to reduce this pressure that the Anglo-French offensive in Picardy was brought forward from September to 1 July 1916.

◆ The Battle of Verdun: part of the defences of Fort Douaumont after a German artillery strike.

▲ French troops take refuge in the stronghold of Fort Douaumont. French casualties at Verdun would reach an incredible 300,000 by August 1916.

▼ Fort Douaumont from the air, February 1916, showing the effects of German shelling. The fort fell shortly after the picture was taken.

◀ Marshal Philippe Petain, the hero of Verdun.
Appointed commander in February, Petain halted
the German advance and held the French line
throughout 1916.

➤ German infantry mount an attack at Verdun, winter 1916. Verdun would cost the Germans dear in their
attempt to 'bleed the French white'.

▸ Cutting the French barbed wire at Verdun, prior to yet another German assault.

⬤ French dead in a trench beyond Fort Vaux, Verdun. Fort Vaux would hold out against attack after attack until it was finally captured on 7 June 1916.

☛ A fallen French soldier's rifle and helmet make a poignant grave marker, Verdun, 1916.

The Battle of the Somme

The plan was a simple one: Fourth Army, under the command of General Sir Henry Rawlinson, was to advance 1½ miles along a 14-mile wide front. Reserve Army (later renamed Fifth Army, under General Sir Hubert Gough, would then advance through the gap, capture the town of Bapaume, and then swing north towards Arras, rolling up the enemy trenches as it went. In the event, things did not go quite according to the plan.

ARTILLERY BOMBARDMENT

The artillery bombardment that preceded the attack began on 24 June, and would last for the entire week until 1 July: long enough, it was estimated, to cut the German wire, destroy most of their front-line positions, and generally demoralise any troops it failed to kill. For a number of reasons, including a shortage of shells, local variations in the strength and duration of the bombardment, and the fact that the German lines held a number of deep bunkers unaffected by

▲ Aerial view of the Somme battlefield, July 1916. The British troops in the foreground are advancing on the German positions to the rear of the remnants of the small wood. This photograph reveals all too clearly the devastation caused to farm and woodland by artillery.

the shelling, the bombardment did not achieve all of its aims. Hence when battle opened on 1 July, troops in many areas found the barbed wire in front of them intact, leaving them exposed to the German machine guns as they tried desperately to cut their way through. Success, which came essentially south of the Albert–Bapaume road, was often due to individual commanders on the ground. The men of 97th Brigade of 32nd Division, for example, had moved into No Man's Land before the end of the bombarment, and were thus on the spot to rush the German trenches, and to capture the stronghold named the Leipzig Redoubt. Their sister brigade, the 96th, followed exactly the tactics laid down in the manuals, and were wiped out. By midnight on 1 July, objectives had been reached and even passed in some areas south of the Albert-Bapaume road: north of this road, however, where the concentration of German guns was higher, and the defences deeper, the success rate was alarmingly small. The total number of casualties suffered by the British on the first day of the Somme was 57,470, including 20,000 dead. It was and remains the bloodiest day in the history of the British army.

◆ British infantry in the firing line fix bayonets as they prepare to advance across No-Man's Land at the Battle of Albert, July 1916.

➦ General Sir Henry Rawlinson, commander of the British Fourth Army. One of the more able and innovative generals of the First World War, Rawlinson's reputation has suffered as a result of the British losses on the Somme.

☞ French 370mm howitzer prepares to open fire at Ravin de Proyart, during the Battle of the Somme.

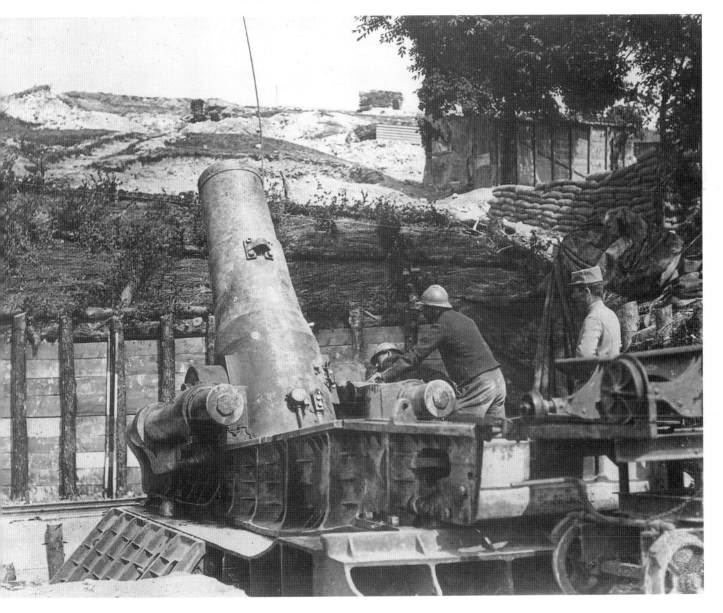

◗ Artillery shell explodes on the Somme. The impact of millions of artillery shells was to turn the land into a quagmire.

☛ Used shell cases, September 1916 are a mute testament to the intensity of artillery fire on the Western Front during the Battle of the Somme.

◆ British poster, aimed at recruiting women into the armaments factories, 1916. The massive amounts of shells used by the British during their bombardments preliminary to an attack proved very difficult to keep up with.

▲ Wiring party of the Royal Warwickshire Regiment advances to the front line, Beaumont Hamel, July 1916.

☛ British and German wounded make their way to a dressing station near Bernafay Wood, 19 July 1916, during the Battle of Bazentin Ridge.

INCHING FORWARD

The advance continued, however, albeit at a far slower speed, and with a far higher casualty rate than had been anticipated by even the pessimists on the British general staff. By the end of July, the Germans had been pushed back all across the battlefront, and towns such as La Boisselle, Ovilliers and Pozieres were once more in Allied hands. Some of the success of the first day had been due to a new artillery tactic known as the creeping barrage, where the line of shelling moves steadily forwards, with the infantry following closely behind. The battle of Flers-Courcelette on 15 September would see another British innovation, the tank, capture the village of Flers. Although only 32 tanks were committed at Flers, considerably lessening their impact, with their aid the British succeeded in capturing twice the ground taken on 1 July, at a cost of less than half the casualties. Although not yet the wonder weapon hoped for, the tank had demonstrated its potential at Flers.

⬥ Abandoned German trench at Delville Wood, during the battle there, September 1916.

The British continued to inch their way forward across the muddy wastes, and by 7 October had recaptured the key town of Le Sars. With the capture by Gough's Fifth Army of Beaumont Hamel and Beaucourt on the north bank of the Ancre on 13 November, in a day of savage fighting, Haig decided that that was as good as it got, and the Battle of the Somme was closed down on 19 November.

The end result of four and a half months of bitter fighting was the gain of a strip of muddy ground 6 miles by 20, at a cost of some 400,000 British and Dominion casualties, including Australians, New Zealanders, Indians and Canadians. The cost was appallingly high: however, the German front line had been broken, the pressure on the French had been relieved, allowing them to recapture the ground lost to the German Verdun offensive, and it had cost the Germans some 600,000 casualties.

▲ Soldiers of the Wiltshire Regiment advancing to the attack at Thiepval, at the northern end of the Somme battlefield, August 1916. The town was finally taken by the British in September.

🔺 Gas-masked men of the British Machine Gun Corps, during the British Somme offensive of 1916 with Vickers machine gun. The Vickers was found to be impractically heavy, and would be replaced with the Lewis gun during the course of 1916–17.

☛ Troops of the Border Regiment rest in a front line trench at Thiepval Wood, August 1916. Recruited from the rugged hill country of Westmorland and Cumberland in the north of England, the men of the Borders were renowned for their hardiness, and were probably better able than most troops to cope with the rigours of life in the trenches.

▶ British second wave troops move up in support of the first line of attack, Battle of Morval, September 1916.

▲ Fourteenth Army HQ, 12 September 1916. General Haig, together with General Joffre, makes his point to David Lloyd George, British Prime Minister. The relationship between Haig and Lloyd George, never cordial, would deteriorate considerably throughout the war.

▶ Fix bayonets: Canadian troops prepare to go 'over the top' in the Somme area, October 1916. The Canadian contribution to the Allied effort during the First World War was huge. Just ten weeks after war was declared, the 1st Canadian Division was underway to Europe. In April 1915 the Canadians held the line at Ypres, in the face of the German gas attacks, as French Colonial troops on their flank broke and ran. The Canadian Corps was also strongly represented on the killing-fields of Passchendaele in 1917, but it is their capture of Vimy Ridge in the first wholly successful Allied attack of the war that remains their most enduring legacy.

⬥ Kaiser Wilhelm hands out medals behind the Somme battlefield, 1916.

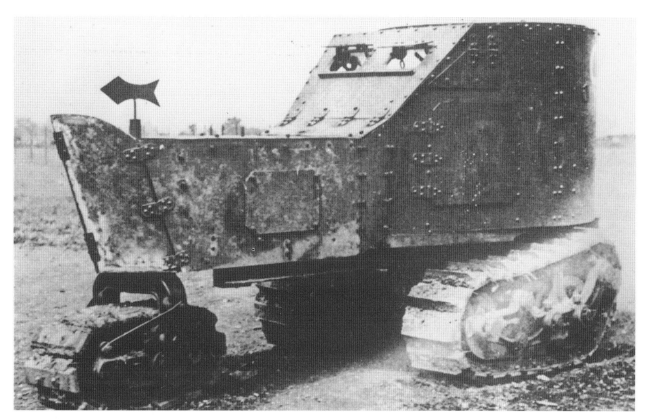

◆ Prototype armoured tractor, manufactured by Killen-Strait, and claimed to be the first completed tank, shown here in 1915. Although the basic principles are present, i.e caterpillar tracks, and armour, the tank had a long development still ahead of it.

◆ British Mark I tank in action at Thiepval, 25 September 1916. The version shown is a 'male' version, i.e it has six-pounder guns mounted in the sponsons on its sides. The 'female' versions were armed with machine guns. Note also the trailing wheel at the rear of the tank, soon discarded as serving no particular purpose. The wood and chicken-wire structure on the top of the tank, intended as an anti-grenade device, was also soon discarded, on the grounds that it caused more problems than it solved.

◆ *D17*, Mark I tank, at Flers, 17 September 1916. Tanks had played a vital role in taking the town of Flers two days previously, in their first appearance on a battlefield.

➡ *D17* at Flers, performing its new role as a Brigade headquarters.

➤ Knee deep in mud on the Lesboeuf Road outside Flers, horses struggle to pull an artillery limber loaded with ammunition up to Flers, November 1916.

The Death of Lord Kitchener 5 June 1916

As Secretary of State for War in August 1914, Lord Kitchener had not shared the majority view the war would be quickly over. Accordingly, he had begun a recruiting campaign, calling for 100,000 volunteers. In three weeks he had them, and before the end of the year, Kitchener's 'New Army' stood in excess of one million, men who were to prove vital to the continuance of the war in 1916.

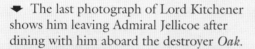 The last photograph of Lord Kitchener shows him leaving Admiral Jellicoe after dining with him aboard the destroyer *Oak*.

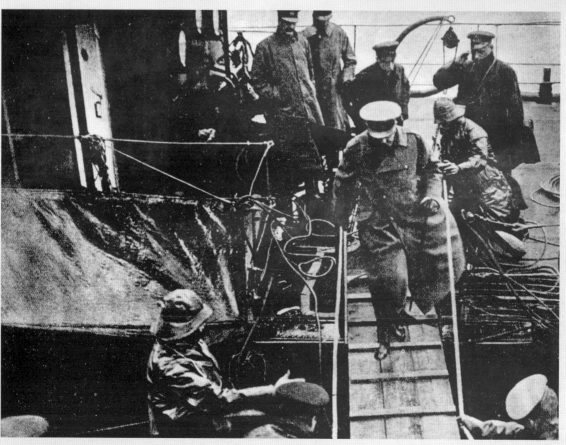

Kitchener was bound for Russia from Scapa Flow on 5 June 1916 aboard the destroyer *Hampshire* when she struck a mine in the Baltic Sea and sank with the loss of all hands. Kitchener had become a potent symbol of the British will to fight, as embodied by his famous posters declaring that 'Your Country Needs You', and his passing was mourned by the nation.

◀ Lord Kitchener of Khartoum. A successful commander in India in the early twentieth century, Kitchener had proved his abilities as a soldier in the nineteenth in Egypt, particularly at the Battle of Omdurman. He became the first serving soldier to also serve as Secretary of State for War, on his appointment to the post in August 1914.

➡ News headline announces Kitchener's death, June 5 1916.

Year of Changes

The Middle East

BRITISH TROOPS HAD BEEN sent to the Middle East as early as 1914, to protect the oilfields from any potential attack by Turkey. Kut was captured after the Turkish declaration of war, but was then besieged by the Turks from December 1915, finally capitulating due to lack of food and water in April 1916. By February 1917 it was back in British hands, however, and by the following month British troops had entered Baghdad.

In early 1917, General Sir Edmund Allenby was transferred from the Western Front and given command of the British forces in Palestine. Sweeping through the Sinai from Egypt and up through the future Israel, Allenby won notable victories at Gaza in March and Beersheba in October. On 11 December 1917, Allenby reached the city of Jerusalem, entering on foot to avoid emulating the triumphal 1898 horseback entrance of the German Kaiser. The Middle

➤ General Sir Edmund Allenby. After commanding the British Third Army on the Somme, Allenby was transferred to the Middle Eastern theatre early in 1917. Under Allenby, the British won a string of victories throughout 1917 that saw them occupy Jerusalem in December. British forces would eventually reach Aleppo near the Turkish border by October 1918 and force the Turks to sue for peace.

Eastern campaign was put on hold during the German spring advances of 1918, but by May Allenby's forces were underway once more, as were the Arab forces of the Sherif of Mecca, led by an Englishman, T.E Lawrence, Lawrence of Arabia. On 1 October, Lawrence and Allenby reached the city of Damascus, where the Turks had taken refuge, and captured the town, taking over 20,000 Turks prisoner. Beirut fell to the British the following day, and by 25 October 1918, Allenby's forces had taken Aleppo, close to the southern Turkish border. The Turks sued for peace, and an armistice was signed on 30 October, 11 days before the German signing. The campaign in the Middle East was over.

➤ Australian cavalry move into the attack at the Battle of Gaza, March 1917.

➤ T.E. Lawrence, 'Lawrence of Arabia'. Lawrence was an archaeologist employed by British Intelligence at the outbreak of the First World War to produce maps of the Arab region, an area of which he had detailed knowledge. He went with the British Mission to aid the Sherif of Mecca in his revolt against the Ottoman Empire, and organised his army into an efficient fighting force against the Turks. He reached Damascus at the head of his troops, hours before Allenby's forces on 1 October 1917.

⬆ British entry into Baghdad with Turkish prisoners under escort. British forces under Major General Sir Frederick Maude captured the city in March 1917.

⬇ British forces under Major General Allenby enter Jerusalem, 11 December 1917.

↞ Soldiers of a Russian Women's 'Death' battalion take the oath.

The collapse of the Eastern Front

In March 1917, following severe civil unrest and the creation of Soviets – revolutionary councils composed of workers, soldiers and parliament members – the Tsar abdicated, and a provisional government was formed under Prince Lvov. The new government lasted just two months, when a new provisional government under Prime Minister Alexander Kerensky was formed and took over the conduct of the war. In an offensive beginning on 1 July, one year exactly after the British attack on the Somme began, the Kerensky offensive opened along a front stretching from Tarnopol in the north to beyond Czernowitz in the south. Despite initial success, the German response was too much for the crumbling Tsarist army, however, and on 7 November, the Bolsheviks led by Vladimir Lenin, a drifting political thinker returned to Russia by the Germans in the hope that he would do exactly that, seized control. A delegation was immediately sent to discuss an armistice with the Germans, which was eventually signed on 3 March 1918 at Brest-Litovsk, and which handed over vast swathes of Russian agricultural land to the Germans. The treaty was far harsher than that of Versailles would be in 1918 to the defeated Germans, a fact conveniently overlooked in an embittered post-war Germany. With the Russians now out of the war, German troops were freed for the massive offensives which would be mounted almost immediately on the Western Front in the spring of 1918.

☚ Scenes from a Revolution: Crowds mass outside the Kremlin in Moscow, October 1917: Trotsky and Stalin (in the hat) are on a podium to the right of the picture (above) while Petrograd workers (inset, right) prepare to open fire on Tsarist troops.

(left inset) Vladimir Lenin addresses a crowd on the first anniversary of the Revolution, November 1918. Lenin was the first Premier of Russia, after the Bolshevik October Revolution deposed the provisonal government of Alexander Kerensky, 1917. The Bolsheviks immediately sued for peace with Germany, signing an armistice in March 1918.

The Western Front

THE ARRAS OFFENSIVE

On Easter Monday, 9 April Lieutenant General Sir Julian Byng's Canadian Corps launched an attack on the ridge beyond the town of Vimy, north of Arras, while a simultaneous attack was launched around Arras itself by elements of General Allenby's Third Army. The Canadian attack captured Vimy Ridge on 9 April, taking 4,000 German prisoners, and pushing the German lines back over 2 miles: the cost was so high, however, 10,000 casualties, including almost 4,000

▶ German shelling during the Battle of Arras at Monchy-le-Preux, April 1917. The British dugout in the foreground is serving as a dressing station, while in the middle of the picture are British field guns.

➡ Arras, 29 April 1917. A British military band plays in what was once the main square of the town, but is now reduced to rubble by artillery fire.

dead, that British generals took the unprecedented step of protesting to General Haig, who concurred. The attack beyond Arras also met with success, with British troops reaching the third German line of trenches within the first few hours. This line held however, and the attacks gradually ran out of steam; on 15 April, Haig declared the offensive over. The British and Canadians had achieved a measure of success, if at high costs; the same could not be said for the French Nivelle Offensive, launched on 16 April, as the Battle of Arras was coming to an end.

☛ Barbed wire entanglements near Heninel forming part of the Hindenburg Line defences, May 1917.

➤ British cavalry in Arras during the Battle of Vimy Ridge, April 1917. The long-awaited chance for a cavalry breakthrough never appeared, however.

➤ Men of the 29th Infantry Battalion advance across No Man's Land toward the Vimy Ridge under heavy German fire, 9 April 1917. The ridge was taken the same day.

◆ Canadian troops of 19th Infantry Battalion, belonging to General Sir Julian Byng's Canadian Corps dig themselves in on the top of Vimy Ridge.

◗ German prisoners captured during the battle for the Vimy Ridge, April 1917.

☛ Canadian machine gunners take up their positions on the Vimy Ridge.

☛ Canadian troops constructing plank roads to allow heavy traffic to pass following the successful battle of Vimy Ridge.

The Vimy memorial. Standing on land given to the Canadian people in perpetuity by the French nation, the Vimy memorial is a fitting remembrance of the 11,000 Canadian troops who died taking the ridge.

The Nivelle Offensive

This was launched on 16 April, with the intention of capturing the Chemin des Dames, the road which ran behind the German lines on the north bank of the Aisne. Although the French Fifth and Sixth Armies made small gains, the attack was a disaster. In the wake of the 190,000 casualties suffered by the French, the army decided that enough was enough and mutinied. Nivelle was replaced by the hero of Verdun, Marshal Philippe Petain, who ruled out any more large scale French offensives, despite the fact that it was French territory the Germans were occupying. With the French out of action, the onus was thrown onto the British army to keep the attacks going, which they did, first at Messines in June, and then, infamously, to the west of Ypres, at the little Belgian village of Passchendaele.

French medical unit tends a wounded comrade, April 1917.

☛ Second wave of a French attack on the Chemin des Dames by II Colonial Corps of Sixth Army during the Nivelle Offensive, April 1917.

☛ German sharpshooters move forward along the River Aisne, April 1917.

PASSCHENDAELE

The reasons for an attack in the area around Passchendaele were manifold: it would eliminate the risk of a German breakthrough to the ports of Dunkirk and Nieuport; it offered the British a chance of breaking through to the Belgian ports of Ostend and Zeebrugge, denying these to the German U-boats; it was close to the British supply lines, and, if the German positions were taken, it offered the chance of rolling up the German line from north to south.

The attack began with the launching of the assault on the Messines Ridge by British and Anzac troops on 7 June, prefaced by the detonation of 21 enormous mines, the effects of which were felt as an earthquake in England, and thoroughly dazed and confused the Germans. The ridge was taken the same day, and the operation, despite German counter-attacks, was one of the most successful to be launched up until that point. The gains were not followed up until 31

◆ Storming German concrete strongholds at the Battle of Messines, 7 June 1917. The offensive was one of the more successful Allied efforts, helped by the explosion of huge mines underneath the German positions before commencing the attack, and the use of a highly effective creeping artillery barrage, controlled by Major Alan Brooke, the future Chief of the Imperial General Staff of the British Army during the Second World War.

July, however, a disastrous decision, given that the Germans knew there was an attack in the offing, and, more importantly, knew where the attack would be launched.

By the time the battle at Passchendaele, the Third Battle of Ypres, was finally launched the Germans were ready. The month-long British bombardment that had preceded the attack had turned the ground into one vast sea of mud into which men and horses disappeared without trace, severely hindering any advance. Although the Germans were pushed back and limited gains were made, the battle was to continue far too long, until 6 November, under intolerable conditions. Although Passchendaele was captured, and the aim of the battle therefore at least partially achieved, the cost in casualties, around 250,000, was unacceptably high. Ultimately, all the ground so arduously and so gallantly fought for and captured would be lost to the Germans once again the following spring.

☚ The view across the Douve Valley, with a British artillery bombardment of Messines in progress during the Battle of Messines Ridge, June 1917.

← British and Anzac troops study a contour map of the Wytschaete area, 6 June 1917 prior to the successful Allied attack.

✦ German prisoners taken during the battle of the Messines Ridge, 8 June 1917.

✦ German trenches captured by the British in the Oosttaverne Wood in the Messines region.

◗ British 60-pounder guns in action near Langemarck during the Third Battle of Ypres, 12 October 1917. The whole area has become the massive sea of mud so often associated with the trench warfare of the Western Front. Passchendaele was as bad as it could get.

◀ In the firing line at Passchendaele during the Third
Battle of Ypres, July 1917.

⬥ Stretcher bearers of the 2nd Division, including two German POWs, prepare to evacuate a wounded comrade, Passchendaele, October 1917.

➥ 14 November 1917 Soldiers of the 16th Canadian Machine Gun Regiment using shell holes as makeshift defences at Passchendaele Ridge.

The Air War

Although the Battle of Cambrai is best known for its massed tank assault, an important part was also played by the British RFC, the Royal Flying Corps, who acted as artillery spotters, and also harassed German troops on the ground.

At the beginning of the First World War, aircraft were essentially a new and untried invention, as least as far as the military were concerned. The first aerial sorties were bombing raids carried out on Belgian and British towns by the German airships, the Zeppelins. By 1915, however, aircraft were becoming more widely used, for reconnaissance and for artillery registration. By the middle of 1915, single-seater aircraft had been fitted with machine guns with a timing mechanism that allowed them to fire through the arc of the propellor, and the emphasis began to shift to single combat between individual pilots, or more usually, squadrons of pilots.

The German air force would remain generally dominant in terms of aircraft and manpower almost throughout the war, until the arrival of new British planes such as the Bristol fighter, the SE5 and the Sopwith Camel meant the RFC could compete on more level terms with the Fokkers and Albatrosses.

➤ Baron Manfred von Richthofen, the Red Baron. The highest-scoring ace of the war, he was finally shot down by Canadian Captain Arthur Brown on 21 April 1918. His Fokker made a perfect landing behind Allied lines, but when Australian troops ran to investigate, they found him dead at the controls.

In 1918, the Royal Flying Corps became an independent service arm, and was rechristened the Royal Air Force. By 1918, aircraft were becoming more integrated into general offensives, as had been seen at Cambrai in November of the previous year, and this integration reached its height by the time the Allied offensives of later 1918 began. The RAF was an essential part of the great Allied advance from Amiens, and this coordination would continue to develop even after the war had ended.

Allied 'aces' – pilots or gunners with 5 or more 'kills' to their credit – included the Canadians William Bishop and Raymond Collishaw, with scores of 72 and 60 respectively, Frenchmen Rene Fonck and Georges Guynemer, with 75 and 54 respectively, and British pilots Edward Mannock with 61, and Albert Ball, with a total of at least 44 in just twelve months at the front.

German aces included Ernst Udet, with a total of 62, and Erich Löwenhardt with 54. Perhaps the best-known pilot of the First World War is Baron Manfred von Richthofen, the 'Red Baron', named for the blood-red Fokker Dr.1 triplane which he flew, the leader of *Jagdgeschwader Richthofen*, the Richthofen Circus. His total of 80 aircraft shot down was the highest of the war.

➤ Members of Richthofen's famous 'Circus' squadron pose for the camera, France, 1917.

◀ English air ace Albert Ball. In his 12 months at the front, Ball succeeded in shooting down 44 enemy aircraft, a phenomenal rate of success. He was shot down and killed during a dogfight with members of Richthofen's Circus in May 1917, aged just twenty.

☛ Sopwith Camel. Named the Camel after the humped fairing covering its twin machine guns, the Camel was an agile, highly manoeuvrable biplane credited with destroying 1,294 enemy aircraft, more than any other Allied aircraft during the war. The Camel was also an extremely difficult aircraft to fly, and became infamous for the death toll it exacted on the inexperienced, the unwary or the forgetful. During the First World War, 413 pilots died in combat and 385 pilots died from non-combat related causes while flying the Sopwith Camel.

◆ Aces high: British SE5s fight it out with German Fokker D-VIIs.

Cambrai

1917 on the Western Front came to an end with the battle of Cambrai on 20 November, the first massed tank attack in history. Initially successful, the British attack at Cambrai ground to a halt due to an inability to exploit initial gains made, the perennial problem of the Western Front, caused at least in part by the immobility of the artillery, poor communications, and at Cambrai, the inability of one divisional commander to grasp the nature of tank-infantry co-operation. Although the advance went further than previously, the German line held, enabling them to launch counter-attacks, which soon encountered the same difficulties as the initial British attacks.

The Battle of Cambrai was essentially a stalemate: German losses would be harder to replace than those of the Allies, but the tactics of both sides were showing success. As more and more US soldiers began arriving in France, however, the balance had begun to tilt to the side of the Allies.

⬥ Air and tank battle, Cambrai, November 1917. The heads of German soldiers can be seen on the right of the picture.

▶ Tanks are brought up by train in preparation for the attack on Cambrai, November 1917. The tanks carry fascines, huge bundles of brushwood which are dropped into enemy trenches, enabling the tanks to cross over.

➡ British tanks of G Battalion, 40th Division pass captured German guns at Graincourt on the way to the attack on Bourlon Wood, 23 November 1917.

The Italian Front

On the Italian Front, the attack by the Central Powers at Caporetto had been a disaster for the Italians, who were pushed back to the line of the Piave river, and took heavy casualties. Altogether, the Central Powers had had a generally successful year. With the Russians suing for peace, it was no longer necessary to fight on two fronts; the Italians were in retreat; the French had mutinied and were effectively on hold as a fighting force. Two things gave cause for concern, however: firstly, the British had achieved successes in the field, albeit at higher cost than they would have liked, and the BEF was becoming numerically stronger and an increasingly effective fighting force. Secondly, the USA had entered the war.

⬥ Austro-Hungarian grenadiers on the Isonzo Front, September 1917, at the beginning of the offensive that would see the Italian front line crumble.

◀ Italian troops surrender to the attacking Austrians near Flitsch on the Isonzo front, October 1917.

➡ Italian casualties lie where they have fallen in their trench on the Heights of Tolmine during the Battle of Caporetto, 1917.

◆ Italian troops give themselves up, October 1917.

◆ Victims of a German grenade attack on a pass between
Flitsch and Tolmine, October 1917.

➤ German photograph showing a destroyed Italian ammunition column at the Battle of Caporetto, November 1917.

◆ The Italian retreat from the Isonzo front, November 1917. They would halt and hold the German-Austrian advance along the line of the Piave river north of Venice.

◆ Italian retreat to the Piave, November 1917.

The United States goes to war

There were two principal reasons behind the US Declaration of War, the most immediate being the 'Zimmerman telegram', a message sent by the German Foreign Secretary, Arthur Zimmerman, to the German ambassador in Mexico, suggesting the possiblity of a military alliance between Germany and Mexico in the event of a US declaration of war. This was picked up by British Naval Intelligence and passed on to an understandably outraged US government. The second and more long-standing cause of the US entry into the war was German submarine attacks on US merchant ships. Although President Wilson had warned the Germans of the likely US reaction to attacks on its shipping, Germany had gambled that the British would be defeated before the US had a chance to mobilise, and ship its army over to Europe. The Kaiser lost his gamble: on 6 April 1917, the USA declared war on Germany.

American mobilisation was swift; by July the National Guard had been mobilised, conscription was in force, and the 125,000 strong American Expeditionary Force, under the command of General John Joseph Pershing, a veteran of the Mexican wars had begun to arrive in France, the first troops landing on 25 June. The US contribution would eventually rise to over 2 million front line troops by November 1918, around one third of the total Allied strength. Faced with the prospect of US military muscle, and almost limitless industrial potential, Hindenburg and Ludendorff knew that if victory on the Western Front were to come, it would have to come soon.

▶ President Woodrow Wilson. Initially committed to US neutrality, Wilson became increasingly angered by the unrestricted submarine warfare being waged by the Germans. He also recognised that German imperial interests would eventually threaten those of the USA.

🔺 The US declaration of war on Germany is read out
to a packed Congress, 6 April 1917. America's entry
into the war would prove decisive in bringing the war
to an end during 1918.

➤ General John Joseph Pershing, commander of the newly-formed American Expeditionary Force, seen here reviewing a guard of honour at Boulogne, May 1917.

US troops parade through London on their way to France, August 1917.

American soldier shakes hands with a youthful member of the watching public as his troop parade through the streets of London, 15 August 1917.

US troopship begins to unload in France.

The first US troops arrive in France.

➤ US troop train on its way to the front lines, France 1917.

Year of Victories

AS WE HAVE SEEN, 1917 closed with a defeat for Italy, the retirement of Russia from the war, the French army in mutiny and the British involved in successful assaults which had nevertheless descended into demoralising slogging matches. That an Allied victory would come in less than a year would have seemed highly unlikely to anyone: indeed, Allied commanders were laying plans for offensives in 1919, and in some cases, planning for as far ahead as 1920. The Americans in particular, were of the opinion that the war would not be over quickly, and were planning accordingly; that General Pershing did not in fact get his 100 divisions in France was due to the war ending before he had anticipated.

The US declaration of war on Germany in April 1917 was one bright spot in the year for the Allies. Although it did not necessarily guarantee an Allied victory – the US Army was still small and relatively untried in 1917 – it did shift the balance in the Allies' favour, and the German High Command knew it.

While the British had taken measures to make sure the civilian population was taken care of, by such means as a concerted centralised propaganda effort and the introduction of rationing, to encourage a 'we're all in it together' mentality, the Germans had failed to do so. With the country a virtual military dictatorship, it was perhaps inevitable that the army's needs would come first, and this would lead to increasing civilian unrest as the war progressed, and the British blockade began to bite. The problems on the home front, combined with the severe losses suffered by the German troops during the attritional battles of 1917, and the need to keep up

➥ Big Bertha, one of the giant railway guns used by the Germans to shell Paris during May and June, 1918. The city suffered more than 500 casualties, including over 200 killed.

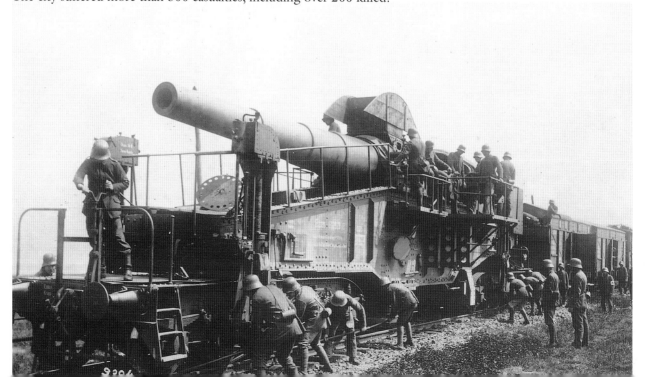

The German High Command; Hindenburg, Kaiser Wilhelm II and Ludendorff, confer. The offensives launched by the German army in the spring of 1918 were largely the brainchild of Ludendorff, increasingly senior in the partnership with Hindenburg. After the war the Kaiser would go into exile, while Ludendorff would take part in the risible putsch attempt by Adolf Hitler in Munich 1923, and sit in the Reichstag as a Nazi member, eventually becoming disillusioned with his Führer. Paul von Hindenburg went on to be elected President and in 1933 he would commit one of the worst errors of judgement in the history of the world when he appointed Hitler as Chancellor of Germany. 'Future generations,' Ludendorff informed him on hearing this news, 'will damn you in your grave for what you have done.'

to 50 divisions on the Eastern Front, even after the Russian peace negotiations had begun, meant that the German position was anything but secure. When the manpower and equipment that the USA would soon begin to provide was taken into account, the position was precarious indeed. Ludendorff knew that if Germany were to stand a chance of winning the war, it would have to be before the Americans began arriving in France, and while the British and the French were still recovering from their exertions of 1917. It was time for the German Army to go back over to the offensive.

The German Spring Offensives, 1918

These began with Operation *Michael*, aimed at the British positions at Arras, the 'hinge' between the BEF and the French Army. The intention was to break through here, thus separating the British from the French, and then roll up the British line from north to south.

The offensive opened on 21 March, at 0930 hours, and its initial success was enormous, as the 750,000 attackers confronted the fewer than 300,000 British defenders. By the end of the day, the Germans had pushed the British front line back 17 miles, to the line of the Crozat Canal, and taken around 20,000 prisoners. By 5 April, the British were defending a line just 10 miles to the east of Amiens, and the whole of the Somme region, so hard won in 1916, was in German hands. The British had made an orderly retreat, however; they were now reinforced by French reserves, and the Germans had exhausted their strength seizing ground of no strategic significance. The British line held firm. Ludendorff switched his attention to Flanders, attacking the Ypres salient yet again on 9 April, aiming to seize the railway junction at Hazebrouck, and push through to the Channel coast. This attack was halted just 5 miles east of Hazebrouck, the gravity of the position reflected in General Haig's now famous order of the day for 11 April:

> *Every position must be held to the last man. There must be no retirement. With our backs to the wall and believing in the justice of our cause, each one must fight on to the end. The safety of our homes and freedom of mankind alike depend upon the conduct of each one of us at this critical moment.*

➧ Transport columns move up to the front near Nesle in preparation for Operation *Michael*, the German offensive in Picardy, March 1918.

Although the ridge at Passchendaele, captured at so high a cost the previous year fell on 25 April, the German advances were running out of steam. At Flanders, they were halted at the Battle of Lys on April 29, while on the Somme the village of Villers-Bretonneux, captured on 24 April, had been retaken the same night by a joint Australian-British attack.

The German offensives in the north had been broken by the British and Dominion troops; now came the turn of the French to the south.

☞ German troops mass in the ruined streets of St Quentin immediately prior to the *Michael* offensive, 21 March 1918.

▶ German storm troops during the Spring Offensive. Storm troops were the elite of the German army, concentrating on achieving a breakthrough of enemy lines and leaving strongholds to be mopped up by the following infantry.

☞ German troops advance through the French town of Bailleuil, April 1918.

➤ German infantry advance over a captured trench during the attack between Montdidier and Noyon, June 1918. The offensive was named Operation *Gneisenau*, and was the follow-up to the stalled *Michael* of March. Montdidier would be as far as the attack in the Somme area would reach.

The AEF in Action

The third German offensive of 1918 came on 27 May, and, due in part to the incompetence of General Denis Duchene, the French army commander in the Soissons-Marne area, succeeded for the third time in taking ground. By the end of May the Germans had captured Chateau-Thierry, and were within 40 miles of Paris itself. At Chateau-Thierry, however, they were halted by elements of the US 3rd Division. The AEF was again in action on 6 June, when it fell to the 2nd Division to hold the attack on Belleau Wood. The US Army was inexperienced, particularly in the type of warfare to be found on the Western Front, and they suffered many logistical and communications problems. At Belleau Wood they suffered a high casualty rate, but nevertheless

◆ British and French troops await the German assault along the River Aisne, north of Courville, 29 May 1918.

◆ German troops cut their way through the French barbed wire and advance towards the Aisne river, May 1918. The attack on the Aisne was the third great German offensive of the year. Although it gained ground, it was of little strategic significance.

held out against the attacking Germans and recaptured the wood. The AEF, however in-experienced it might be, learnt quickly; as the Germans launched their final assault on 15 July, they managed to cross the Marne, but were held by the American 3rd Division, who earned themselves the honorific 'Rock of the Marne'. The ensuing Second Battle of the Marne saw French counter attacks recapture Soissons, and straighten the Allied lines by 6 August.

The Americans were again in action around the St Mihiel salient on 12 September, capturing 15,000 prisoners when the salient collapsed.

On 26 September, 600,000 troops of the AEF were redeployed in the Meuse-Argonne region, where they took part in a joint offensive with the French. The terrain made any advance almost impossible, and the AEF suffered heavy casualties, they nevertheless did advance, taking a number of German strongholds, and were preparing a new offensive in November when the news came through that an armistice had been signed.

◆ German troops assault the village of Embermesnil in the Champagne region of France, May 1918.

▶ German infantry cross the Ailette Canal over makeshift bridges in the region of the Chemin des Dames, June 1918.

◀ A column of French prisoners captured during the Second Battle of the Aisne are marched along the Soissons-Fismes Road, June 1918. The huge numbers of prisoners captured in the great offensives of 1918 would become a logistical headache for both sides.

▶ German advance along the road from Courville-Augny, Chemin des Dames, June 1918.

◆ Advance to the front line along the Marne.

◆ Gun crew of 23rd Infantry Regiment of the US 2nd Division in action at Belleau Wood June 1918.

US soldiers inspect a captured German bunker near St Mihiel, 1918.

American machine guns and supply wagons take a break in the ruins of a town, St Mihiel area, September 1918. On 12 September the US captured the German salient around St Mihiel.

◆ US tanks move through the Argonne Forest, 26 September 1918.

◆ US troops move into the Argonne region from St Mihiel, September. The redeployment of 600,000 US troops was a logistical triumph for the AEF, which had developed rapidly throughout the course of the fighting of 1918.

✦ US infantry pause amongst the shattered stumps of what was once a part of the Argonne Forest, October 1918. The area was heavily shelled during what was to become the final US offensive of the war.

☞ Battery 'A' of 108th US Field Artillery in action around Varennes-en-Argonne on the Meuse river, 3 October 1918.

Allied troops man a 14-inch railway gun, October 1918. Guns of this calibre fired a shell weighing 1400 pounds over 20 miles.

The Defeat of the German Army

On 8 August, the British launched an assault on the German positions east of Amiens, in what became known as the Battle of Amiens to the Allies, and 'the black day of the German Army' to Ludendorff. The British advanced 8 miles along a 14-mile front on the first day of the battle, the Germans losing around 27,000 casualties. Although the German army fought on stoically, by mid-September the British had reached the Hindenburg Line and were preparing for their final assault, which began on 29 September. By 4 October, the British had breached the Hindenburg Line, and crossed the two defended canals that formed the Germans' last-ditch defences, finally reaching the open countryside after four long years of trench warfare. Ludendorff's decision that the war could be prolonged led to a public outcry in Germany, and he resigned on 25 October, to be replaced by General Groener. Groener had a far more realistic idea of the way the war was going, and immediately began seeking an armistice with the Allies.

On 4 November Austria-Hungary surrendered at the end of the Battle of Vittoria Veneto, and on the morning of 8 November, a German delegation approached the Allies to begin surrender negotiations. On 9 November, the German Kaiser abdicated, and Germany was declared a republic, with Prince Max of Baden as its First Minister. With the abdication of the Kaiser, the last barrier to peace had gone. An armistice was swiftly agreed, and at 11 a.m. on 11 November, the long years of fighting came to an end. As the church bells in England rang out in celebration, the parents of the poet Wilfred Owen were receiving the telegram informing them of their son's death at the Battle of the Sambre Canal on 4 November. The First World War was over.

◆ German prisoners are escorted to the rear. The men have been captured by members of the Australian 3rd Divisional Pioneers, during the Battle of Hamel, 4 July 1918.

◆ Wounded Canadian troops brought in by gas-masked stretcher bearers at Domart, 9 August 1918. The great Allied offensive to the east of Amiens had begun the day before. British and French tanks, with infantry support from the Australian and Canadian Corps, broke through the German front lines and had advanced to the Hindenburg Line by mid-September.

◆ Allied leaders met at General Joffre's chateau in Beauquesne, August 1918 to discuss their armies' advances. Left to right are: General Joffre, French Commander-in-Chief; Raymond Poincare, President of France; King George V in his uniform of head of the British armed forces; General Foch; General Sir Douglas Haig.

☛ Weary-looking German prisoners captured during the Canadian advance at the Battle of Amiens make their way to the British compound, carrying a wounded comrade, 9 August 1918.

☛ The Battle of Amiens: British Mark V tanks pause for breath in the village of Hourges during the advance 10 August 1918. Seemingly unescorted German prisoners make their way in the opposite direction.

➡ Allied 60-pounder guns open fire on German positions during the Battle of Amiens, 10 August.

 12th Gloucestershires, part of the British 5th Division, advance in artillery formation alongside the road to Achiet-le-Petit, 21 August 1918, as the British continue the push eastwards from Amiens.

 Prisoners captured at Achiet in the taking of the town in August.

◗ 18th Hussars move forward along the undulating ground Courcelles, August. Ridged country such as this, as around Vimy and Messines, for example, proved very hard to take from a well dug-in enemy, the ridges providing a perhaps surprisingly difficult obstacle to overcome.

➨ Australian Field Artillery at Villers-Bretonneux, August 1918 during the Allied Amiens offensive.

➤ German troops surrender to Australians, as they near the Hindenburg Line, September 1918.

◆ Trench forming part of a section of the Hindenburg Line. The Hindenburg Line, or the *Siegfriedstellung* to give it its German title, was a series of strongpoints constructed by the Germans in the autumn and winter of 1916 and reflected their intention of fighting a defensive war in the West while concentrating on offence in the East. Although the British broke through the Line at Arras in 1917 and at Cambrai the following November, they did not follow their successes up, and the Hindenburg Line remained essentially intact until the great Allied offensives of late 1918.

◆ Aerial view of the Hindenburg Line, showing how the trenches were built along zig-zag lines, to prevent enfilading fire. Notice too the impact of shells around the line.

◄ Captured German positions along the Hindenburg Line, October 1918.

◗ Engineers of 4th Division wait for the advance in a captured German trench along the Canal du Nord, September 1918. The Canal du Nord was one of two heavily-defended canals in front of the Hindenburg Line that the Germans hoped would hold out against the British attacks. In fact, British and Canadian troops crossed the Canal du Nord within the first 48 hours of the attack, with the St Quentin canal falling just days later.

➥ Infantry support of 4th Canadian division moves up at the Canal du Nord, following the clearly visible caterpillar tracks left by the advancing British tanks.

◆ Italian troops move forwards over a pontoon bridge across the Piave river, in northern Italy. The Italians had been forced back to the line of the river during the Austrian–German Caporetto assault of November 1917, where they dug in and held the line.

◆ Italian troops at the battle of Vittorio Veneto, November 1918. The Austro-Hungarian army surrendered after the battle on 4 November.

🔺 Paris Peace Conference, January 1918 (l to r)
Prime Minister Vittorio Orlando of Italy; British
Prime Minister David Lloyd George; Prime Minister
of France Georges Clemenceau; President Woodrow
Wilson of the USA. A peace proposal based on
President Wilson's Fourteen Points had been agreed
upon, and offered to the Germans in the summer of
1918. Having rejected the proposal once, the
Germans would have to accept it as the basis of the
November Armistice.

➡ German machine gunners lie where they have fallen, trying to resist an Australian advance near Estrees, October 1918.

◀ Official army telegram received by 'A' Company, 36th Machine-Gun Corps, announcing the date and time of the Armistice. The message appears to have been received at 11.16 a.m. on 11 November, i.e. 16 minutes after the armistice came into force.

◀ Allied leaders gather outside the railway carriage where the Armistice was signed, at Compiegne in France.

▲ Crowds gathered outside Buckingham Palace celebrate the Armistice, November 1918.

◆ V-Day crowds celebrating in Paris.

➥ An American sailor and an American Red Cross nurse, flanked by French soldiers, join the victory celebrations at Vincennes, Paris, November 1918.

➤ Exiled. Recognising that if he remained in power there would be revolution in Germany, the Kaiser finally abdicated, accepting an offer from the Dutch to take up exile in Doorn, Holland. Despite the feeling of many on the Allied side that he should be tried as a war criminal, the Dutch refused to extradite him. He was reunited with his army, however, when it invaded Holland in 1940. The Kaiser died in 1941.

▶ Allied officers stand on chairs outside the Hall of Mirrors at Versailles, eager to witness the signing of the Peace Treaty, 28 June 1919. The Hall of Mirrors had been the setting for the proclamation of the German Empire in 1871; it was perhaps fitting that it should witness its death.

Versailles and beyond

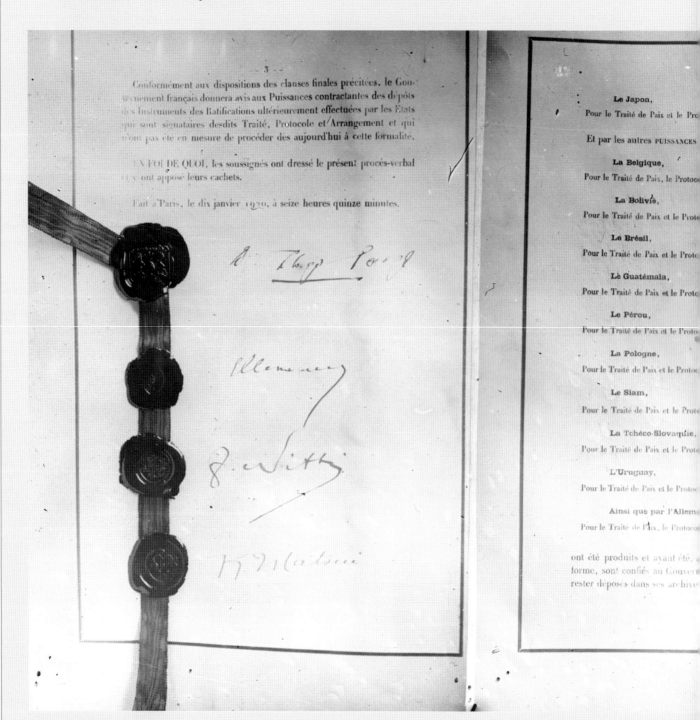

⬆ Signatures on the Versailles Peace Treaty. Negotiations began in January 1919, although the treaty was not finally signed until June the same year, the main sticking point being a German refusal to accept the war guilt clauses the treaty contained. The Treaty has been criticised for being too harsh, particularly in the territory it took from Germany and the demand for reparations, and this harshness has been cited by some historians as a contributory factor to the Second World War. The British Prime Minister Lloyd George had expressed misgivings as to what he perceived as the severity of the Allied demands as early as

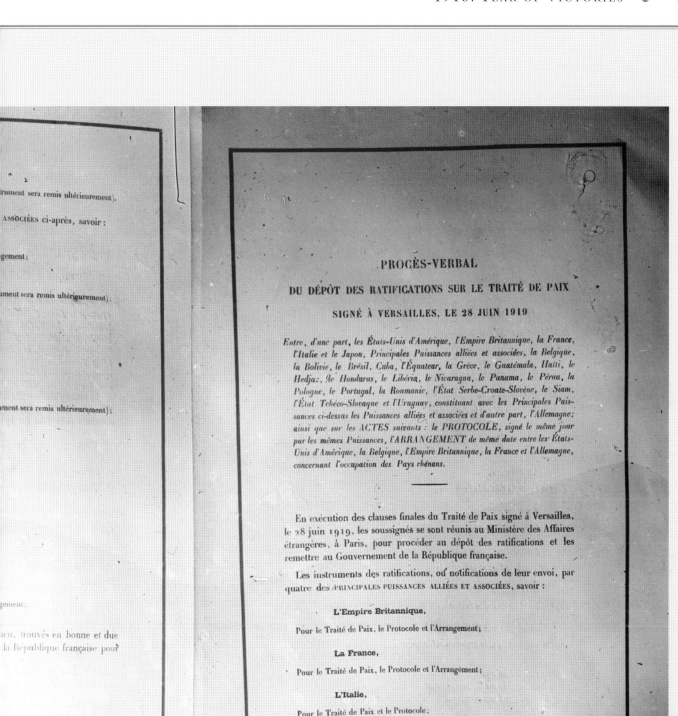

March 1919, and the treaty was rejected by the American Senate on the ground that it was over-harsh. The treaty forced on the Russians at Brest-Litovsk by Germany the previous year, however, makes Versailles seem more than reasonable, and indeed gives a good indication of the sort of terms a defeated France or Britain would have had to expect. The view is also taken by some historians of the war that it was not the harshness of the Versailles conditions, but rather the Allied failure to *enforce* those conditions, that would lead to the Second World War just over twenty years later.

Picture Credits